THE REALITY OF
My Healing

THE REALITY OF
My Healing

*A Personal Reflection on Faith
and God's Delivering Power*

CISLYN TUCKER

Unless otherwise noted, all Scripture quotations are taken from The Holy Bible, King James Version, Public Domain.

Scripture quotations marked NIV are taken from the Holy Bible, New International Version, NIV © 1973, 1978, 1984, 2011 by Biblica, Inc. Used by permission of Zondervan. All rights reserved worldwide. www.zondervan.com

THE REALITY OF MY HEALING
Copyright © 2019 by Cislyn Tucker
SOAR PUBLISHING HOUSE
New York, New York, 11212-9002
www.soarpublishinghouse.com

ISBN 978-1-7332994-1-1 (pbk.)

All rights reserved. No part of this publication may be reproduced, distributed, or transmitted in any form or by any means—electronic, mechanical, digital, photocopy, recording, without the prior written permission of the publisher, except in the case of brief quotations embodied in critical reviews and certain other noncommercial uses permitted by copyright law.

Printed in the United States of America

Contents

Acknowledgements...ix
Introduction...xi

Chapter 1　Instantaneous Healing.................................1
Chapter 2　Tragedy Strikes...10
Chapter 3　Battling through Life....................................17
Chapter 4　Hurricane Katrina...27
Chapter 5　Another Bleeding In the Brain................36
Chapter 6　The Mystery Healing: Brain Tumour...43
Chapter 7　Rebuilt for Ministry: Preaching and
　　　　　　Evangelism..56

Concluding Thoughts...61
A Special Appeal to Unbelievers......................................63
Prayer of Healing...67

*Firstly, I dedicate this book to my one
and only son Javoy Tucker
who loves God with all his heart.
Secondly, to my husband Junior Tucker
who inspired me to write and to be more like Jesus.
Thirdly, it is my deepest desire that this book will
inspire my daughters to surrender their lives totally to God.
Finally, my prayer is that this book will also
challenge, encourage, and inspire readers
to be in a better relationship with God.
May the peace of God, which passes all understanding,
be yours today.*

Acknowledgements

I am eternally grateful to the Holy Spirit, who is the Head of my life. He it was who commissioned me to write this book and gave me its title.

Writing a book was harder than I thought, but more rewarding than I could have ever imagined. None of this would have been possible however, without the invaluable contribution of my best friend, confidante, and greatest critic, my loving husband Junior Tucker. He was patient as well as tolerant to stay up with me into the wee hours of the morning, and even immersed himself into reading early drafts and correcting the manuscripts.

I also want to recognize and express my heartfelt love and appreciation to the following persons without which this book would not be complete and successful.

Thanks to Bishop O'mar Wedderburn who encouraged me to write this book. Thanks to my dear friend, Dr. Kadian Walters for providing much needed guidance and advice for both the book and seminars. Thanks to everyone at Soar

Publishing House. Special thanks to my astute and erudite Editor Ms. Kediesha Watkis.

Thanks to my family who believed in me and stood by me from this book's conception to its completion. I send a special thanks to you all. I have concluded that the only practical way is to set your names down and trust that each person will realize that my gratitude is deep and sincere. I regard and respect everyone for his or her contribution. Your input is indelibly etched on my heart.

Introduction

My life has never been the same since 2005, when I discovered there was a tumour in my brain. I have been a victim of stroke and pulled my way out of numerous seizures. Some people will ask the question "why?" but the answer rests with the Lord Jesus Christ. The record clearly shows that Jesus is the answer (St. John 14:6). Faith in Him has been my sustenance. Between the years 1988 and 2019, God has been doing a tremendous work in my life. I have been battered by sickness, but was able to bounce right back up with the hand of God. Those grievous illnesses that plagued my body brought so much fear into my life; yet I have become closer to God's unchanging grace and experienced His divine intervention. Through it all, I have become stronger, wiser, and better by fighting the good fight of faith.

This book features a series of testimonies drawn from those seasons of my illness. God divinely orchestrated *the reality of my healing*. He turned my life around and sent me to Bible college. I have since devoted myself to the ministry of evangelism, preaching the gospel and winning souls for the kingdom of God. This work is of paramount importance to my life. After all, was it not Jesus, who said in His Word that we are to go into the world and preach the gospel to every creature? (St. Mark 16:15).

Finally, as you read this book, I would like you to know that the supernatural power of God, which has manifested in me, can also be yours today. This same power can transform your life. I now share with you my life-changing testimony.

Chapter 1

INSTANTANEOUS HEALING

Growing up, I would call myself a resilient woman. In many cases, I have learned to withstand and fight against the pressures of life, but at some point, fear tore me apart when I found out that my physical body would no longer be able to function on its own.

I awoke one bright sunny Monday morning in February 1988, when suddenly I felt a pain in my back down to my spine. I went outside trying to do my daily work, but then I began to scream aloud. The pain was unbearable. I rushed into my room where I was alone; all my family members had gone to work. The pain was so severe that I began to scream louder and louder. Fortunately, one of my neighbours was on the same building, and a deacon was visiting that day.

I began screaming more and more as the pain was gushing down my lower back to my feet. I saw my thumbs fall in the middle of the palms of my hands, my tongue was feeling heavy, and I could hardly talk. My feet began to wobble.

I rushed to my neighbour, pounding down the door, screaming. She opened it quickly, looked at me in fright, and cried with a loud voice "JESUS!" The deacon took my right hand and began to pray. He cried aloud to God asking for mercy on me. He shouted loudly and during his prayer, water fell from his eyes onto the palm of my right hand. Immediately, my fingers began to rise again; my tongue was back to normal, and blood was flowing through my toes once more. It was phenomenal, an instantaneous healing! I had not seen anything like this before. I was astonished to see the work of God moving upon my body in seconds.

Shortly after, my mother came and immediately took me to the doctor. Upon examination, he tried his best to characterize the problem, but it was unquestionable. He concluded that I had suffered from a stroke, but he could not say much more about it. In fact, he was astonished how my body overcame a life-threatening condition without any medical help. He was even more surprised to hear when I told him about the supernatural power that took place in the prayer room! All the doctor did was sent me home for bed rest.

It is astounding that man with all his intelligence and knowledge cannot find all the answers, only God can. The incredible God that raised Lazarus from the dead (St John 11:43-44), is the same God who did a miraculous healing in my body. It is necessary for us to acknowledge who He really is. The Bible teaches that Jesus is fully God and fully man (Colossians 2:9; Luke 24:39). He walked the earth and

Instantaneous Healing

did miraculous works–healing the sick, the blind, making the lame to walk again (Luke 5:12). Truly, His power is unmatched.

In my experience, many people think that all healing must be instantaneous; but that may not necessarily be so. Sometimes healing is progressive–it involves a process. With God, healing can sometimes be so sudden that to us it seems almost instantaneous. The important thing and what God's Word promises, is the result, not how long it takes. Many people have given up their faith when they did not have an instant miraculous recovery. Do not let the devil steal from you, through this wrong thinking, what Jesus already paid for you to have!

The Bible tells us that healing is ours, because Jesus paid for it (1 Peter 2:24). However, the Bible never says we will all receive healing instantly. Sometimes it can be very quick— and we know it is a miracle. Other times it can take a while, but no matter how long it takes, we have the promise of God that healing is ours, giving us divine assurance that we will be healthy and whole!

Two stories from the Bible highlight instantaneous healing versus progressive healing.

The first one was Bartimaeus in St. Mark 10:46-52. He was a blind beggar who called out to Jesus for mercy and healing. Bartimaeus' faith was demonstrated when he addressed Jesus as the Son of God. While the crowd told the blind man to be quiet, Bartimaeus just became louder! When Jesus told his disciples to bring the blind man over, the Bible says that *immediately* he received his sight and followed Jesus (verse 52, emphasis added). A miracle happened because of his faith.

St. Mark 8:22-25 gives an account of Jesus ministering to another blind man. After Jesus laid hands on this blind man, he could *"see men like trees, walking."* (verse 24, emphasis added). In other words, he could see, but not very well. Only when Jesus laid hands on him again did his sight become clear. Although a long period was not involved, it does show a healing that involved a *process*—it was not instantaneous. I would like to encourage you, if your healing does not come at once, keep praying and asking in faith, believing that God will come through for you.

Struggle with Fear

During my recovery, even though I marvelled at God's work, fear started to take over my body and I was having doubts about my healing. I began to feel like the pain was still there. Confused and discouraged, I wanted to blame God for my sickness. Although I saw the movement of the Holy Spirit through my body, I still had a doubtful spirit, but realized I had to give this over to God with fasting and prayer.

As I drew closer to Him in obedience, my biggest fear was that my illness would return and it took a tremendous amount of faith and strength to conquer this. For many years, after the first episode in 1988, I used to fear the seizures would come back and with an even greater intensity. I panicked if I did not have the medication. I was anxious whenever the anniversary of my illness came and wondered if it would be a seasonal thing. I was terrified that the tumour in my head would become aggressive and grow. Would there be another bleeding in the brain? Would my heart fail and give up? I feared the possibility of death! It became so unbearable that my body began responding to this fear by causing panic attacks and putting me in a state of hyperventilation, even hysterics. I knew that I was vulnerable, but isn't it true that fear comes at the weakest point of your life? Many people extend their faith to God when they are in distress, difficulties, or a hazardous position. What I have learned is, the more you challenge fear, the more your faith in the Lord grows. It is our responsibility to put fear into God's hand.

My transformation began when I started to renew my mind, according to Romans 12:2. The Bible states in 1 John 4:18 that, "There is no fear in love; but perfect love drives out fear..." God loves me unconditionally, wholeheartedly and continually. I have found comfort in these verses and in these words hundreds of times. Since then I've continued to believe in God's love, even when I do not see it or feel it and this is a sign of Christian maturity. The more I love Him and demonstrate that reality by loving others, the less I am prey to fear. I have developed a culture of love – giving and receiving love. I can still thank God for His love today and live in this love to stand firm and overcome my fears.

Psalm 31:24 says, "Be of good courage and he shall strengthen your heart, all ye that hope in the Lord." One motive the enemy has is to destroy the work of God. He commands our attention by discouraging us from having faith, and influencing us to do things that are not pleasing to God. The fact is, when discouragement sets in, only God can help us. Only He can erase it out of our lives and build our faith in Him. Our physical bodies may experience trials and temptations but we must plant our faith directly in God without hesitation. The Bible says in James 1:3 that the trying of our faith will bring patience. Therefore, with perseverance and patience we will conquer fear. I can truly say my sufferings caused me to wait patiently and earnestly for God's move in my life.

Walking In Disobedience

Learning the Scriptures and studying the Word, I should have been able to stand firm, but I struggled in my walk with God. I did not respect the foundation He laid for me, and walked in disobedience. After my healing, I returned to my ungodly lifestyle. Instead of being planted in His Word, I had forgotten what the Lord had done for me. I stopped entertaining His presence and started to embrace the party and glamour lifestyle. God was no longer important to me. Even though I used to visit church and prayed too, my heart was not at the right place. I was enjoying the mess of this world, allowing the enemy to crowd my mind. I still did not walk in the integrity of His will for my life, but God who bore my sin upon His shoulders, reminded me of the miraculous works He had done in my life.

Instantaneous Healing

The Bible says in I Corinthians 6 verse 20, "For ye are bought with a price: therefore glorify God in your body, and in your spirit, which are God's." In the early 1990s, what I would call the era of the 'bling' or extravagant lifestyle, and arguably, the era of the popular dancehall movement, I had abused the healing that God gave me to glorify him and instead used it to give credence to the adversary, the devil. I once partied a lot and drank hard liquor with friends; dressed in outfits that left nothing to the imagination, adorned myself excessively with gold earrings, chains, and necklaces. Knives and icepicks, to inflict wounds on others, were a part of my outfit–I never went anywhere without packing one. I was a member of the self-proclaimed "gang of trio" in my family. We were seemingly untouchable.

Conceit was driving me away from God. I never believed I was doing anything wrong. I allowed the devil to take authority in my life and I would not amend my ways. The qualities I read about in the Bible, the Fruit of the Spirit according to Galatians 5: *love, joy, peace, patience, kindness, goodness faithfulness, gentleness, and self-control* were not inside me. Without them, I was nothing, but I did not know that. Disobedience took control of my life. I remember an occasion back in 1994 where after church service that Sunday I could not wait to get my "party groove" on for the evening, to drink and hang out with friends who were no better than I was. As I moved from dancehall to dancehall in the dreaded inner cities more popularly called the "ghettos", partying and drinking, I did not realize that the covering of God was still on my life. I

The Reality of My Healing

was crushed inside but did not realize it. I sought comfort in this lifestyle, but God was setting me up for a mighty breakthrough. I felt like an embarrassment to the Holy Spirit and the Almighty God. Even with all that the Lord had done for me, I lost my way.

I walked in disobedience and turned away from God. I received many dreams about walking with the Lord but I was still doing my own thing. It was either "my way or the highway". I was not fully surrendered to God. I would go to church out of tradition and ritual, but the next day I was on the other side.

On one hand, I was desperate for a new beginning, but on the other hand, I was not willing to let go of the things of the world. I was reluctant to give up that lifestyle. This was nothing but pure spiritual blindness.

What I learned during this time is in accordance with the Word in the Bible-God is full of compassion (Psalm 103:8). He is always there to help me when I fall and to pick me up. Even though I was deeply entrenched in disobedience, God still had a mark upon my life. I would try to dismiss His voice, but my inner preacher, my conscience, would not allow me to. I could not shut out that still small voice. I prayed very often but I was not consistent in my prayer life. I knew that God healed me of my incurable condition, yet it seemed that my desire was to walk in disobedience. I ignored every step to salvation and broke every promise that I made to Him when I was sick. Sin got me deeper and deeper, until tragedy struck my family. It was then that I began taking an honest inventory of my life, identifying areas where there were deficiencies. I purposed in my heart that I would really change.

TRAGEDY STRIKES

On December 25, 1994 my twenty-three-year-old sister, who was my best friend became ill. It was no ordinary sickness. She could not walk because her joints were affected; the doctor suspected lupus. She was sick for four months, and during her illness, I was the one caring for her. I did not leave her bedside. My mother, a dedicated Christian, did not hesitate to fast and pray daily. We were looking for a miracle. We prayed, waiting patiently for answers from God but no response came. I became disoriented when there was no change in her situation.

My sister decided to give her life to the Lord–to walk upright with God. Although there was no change in her condition, our family still held on tightly, exercising faith in God; waiting patiently for a supernatural thing to happen. Nothing extravagant took place. We arranged prayer meetings upon prayer meetings at home, but it seemed the prayers went up the ceiling and came right back down. We could only conclude that God was not hearing our prayers. I was confused and my countenance disturbed to know that her sickness was unbearable. Morning by morning we prayed. I began to blame God for not healing her. It even turned out that the hospital could not keep her. My mother decided to take her home. It was devastating to see my sister that I loved so much, in such pain.

I appealed to the Most High God to render assistance, believing that I could force Him to heal my sister. Moreover, I told God He was unreasonable for not healing her, especially knowing that she was loyal to Him. Day by day, I was worried about her not being healed, but I began to notice that God was removing every fear from her. He gave her a peace of mind.

Finally, I concluded that it was up to God to heal her or take her home. I agreed to leave everything in His hands. He was keeping me all through my weakness. Psalm 54:4 tells us, "Behold, God is mine helper: the Lord is with them that uphold my soul." The bitterness I had in my heart God wiped with compassion. He knew that I was vulnerable, so He kept me. I know that I cannot challenge God because He is greater than I am; however, during that time I allowed the circumstances to overwhelm me. It is not easy to be walking someone through his or her sickness wondering, "what will be the result?" or "what if she dies?"

On April 20, 1995 the church that my family attended, decided to launch a tent crusade on an open field in a popular community. We decided to take my sister there. She could not walk, so we had to carry her. The evangelist prayed fervently for her but there were no changes. We all became discouraged and frustrated. All faith was gone from us. There was not even a little faith left in me. My heart was bitter instead of better and blackened with hate. I again began blaming God. I knew He was the only one with the power to heal her. "Where do I go from here? Why? Can God heal her?" I asked. I did not understand, but the answer lied with the Almighty God. It was very difficult and scary for the family. At the same time, my mother, Mama Jenny still kept the faith going. She never gave up; all through the pain and sorrow, she held her faith, all the while praying. Even in this rough time, this strong woman of God kept Him at the centre of her life.

On Sunday morning April 23, 1995 my sister passed away. Everything on the inside of me dried up. I was totally shipwrecked, searching for my faith but could not find it. I was angry inside knowing that the infinite Father who can cure all diseases, with nothing impossible or too hard for Him, did not answer our prayer. I was disappointed and felt like giving up on God, yet He had a plan.

It took some time, but I came to realize that we do not need to feel insignificant when God does not show up in the way we expected. Rather, let us pause for a moment and see the marvellous things God has done secretly for us. We do not know our future and if we were able to see it, many of us would be walking with caution, girting ourselves with salvation. Everybody would like to know the plan that God has for him or her, but Jeremiah 29:11 reveals it all, "For I know the thoughts I think toward you, saith the Lord, thoughts of peace, and not evil, to give you an expected end." You may be feeling the same way I did. I am encouraging you to hold fast to the profession of your faith (Hebrews 9:10). God will lift you up and strengthen you to face the terror that you are exposed to in this sinful world.

Matthew 11:28 tells us, "Come unto me all ye that labour and are heavy laden, and I will give you rest." Throughout our lives, turbulence will come, but we are able to stand firm in the abundance of God's grace. When disaster strikes, the child of God may tremble and feel shaken but let us be encouraged from the words of Apostle Paul in 1 Corinthians 16:13, "Watch ye, stand fast in the faith, quit you like men, be strong."

The Rebirth

On April 24, 1995, still overwhelmed with grief, I decided to go to that same crusade where my sister was saved before she died. I was standing outside, jeering, spectating and minding my own business, when I heard the evangelist making an altar call. He kept on pleading and pleading for one more soul to come to God. He could not go on any further. It was as if heaven stood still and God was waiting for me to surrender. The evangelist was travailing in the spirit and it seemed that he would not stop; it was as if he knew that I needed to come.

I cannot explain what happened but I found myself under

the tent at the altar. It was the best decision I made because right there and then, I put down all my shame, bitterness, and hatred for God. I made up my mind to leave all my burdens and problems right there at the altar. It was the last night of the crusade so the church was having water baptism. I was so overwhelmed with a deep sense of joy from within that I decided to get baptized that same night in a way commonly called the *"Eunuch baptism"* supposedly because it was unplanned and spontaneous, a term coined from Acts 8:26-40 about Philip the evangelist, and the Ethiopian eunuch. Right there in that baptismal pool, I was filled with the Holy Ghost, according to Acts 2:1-8. In addition, three of my other sisters received salvation and were baptized too. I could see the joy on Mama Jenny's face. Physically, she lost one daughter, but three were reborn spiritually into the kingdom of God.

It was a difficult time during my bereavement, but I still walked with God. In fact, I found myself growing in the Lord. Conviction brought me to God. Without the conviction of the Holy Spirit, I would have still struggled with the hurt buried inside of me. Thank God for the blood of Jesus. I was convicted and converted and now, I am living in a full and free salvation. I came to God empty and dry as a restless sinner but He did not turn His back on me; instead, He welcomed me with opened arms.

God asked Abraham in Genesis 18:14, "Is anything too hard for the LORD?" Later, Jeremiah gave the answer: "There is nothing too hard for thee." (Jer. 32:17). The death of my sister brought a transformational change in my life. I was no longer walking in disobedience. Thank God because he had removed it. I felt a new joy and had greater faith in God. Romans 8:28 (NIV) says, "And we know that in all things God works for the good of those who love him, who have been called according to his purpose."

The process of transformation in my life began the day after my sister died. I was a rebel and a wretched sinner who was on a self-destructing path. I had called out the sin for what it was– disobedience. Having called it out, I immediately confessed it and asked God for forgiveness, and claimed His promise of complete pardon–"If we confess our sins, he is faithful and just to forgive us our sins and to cleanse us from all unrighteousness" (I John 1:9). I learned that disobedience to God and even to those in authority over you would block the joy, blessings, and inner peace, which God desires for your life. It may be that the gracious Lord allowed the death of my sister in order to give me that mighty breakthrough of being spiritually reborn and overcoming the sin of disobedience.

The Bible teaches in St. Luke 5:32 that He came not to call the righteous but sinners to repentance. The moment I decided to walk with God I realized that I needed to stand firm, walk in His will, and remain in His presence. I began to lose many persons whom I thought were friends and people who were close to me. I no longer had an appetite for the 'bling' and party lifestyle, but a hunger for God. After all, it was Jesus who said, "Blessed are they which do hunger and thirst after righteousness: for they will be filled" (Matt. 5:6).

David said in Psalm 16:11, "Thou wilt show me the path

of life, in His presence there is fullness of joy and at his right hand there are pleasures for ever more." God had put my broken pieces back together again. I once believed that God rejected me, but since I encountered Him, I have been living in the fullness of His Word. I thank God every moment in my life for His grace and mercy toward me. I had disappointed Him many times, and walked away from the truth, but He was good to me even when I was not good to myself.

When Satan used me as trash and left me to die in the pollution of sin, God plucked me out and turned this "trash" into treasure. Each day, like David in 1 Samuels 30:6, I encouraged myself in the Lord and purposed in my heart that I would not accept defeat no matter what circumstance lies ahead; reminding myself that with God's power I am a victor and not a victim. God loves me, even when I was a fugitive, because He has set His love upon me and helped me to find my way back home. I have learned to appreciate every moment I spend with Christ Jesus. There was nothing that I could have done to stop God from loving me. The Bible says, "Let, I pray thee, thy merciful kindness be for my comfort, according to thy word unto thy servant." (Psalm 119:76). Truly, His love has sustained me.

Chapter 3

BATTLING THROUGH LIFE

One bright morning in April 1999, I woke up and suddenly began feeling so very weak that I could hardly stand. My daughter began screaming. I could not focus because the pain was so severe. I could feel myself slowly fainting but could not describe what exactly was happening to me. I felt like breath was leaving my body, but I was persistent to hold on. I was depending on God for strength. What I was experiencing felt so terrifying, but I was encouraging myself in the Lord. My husband had not gone to work, so he rushed out the door immediately to take me to the hospital. There, doctors diagnosed my condition as being a serious one and therefore took the decision to admit me on the ward.

I did not know that I would make it through. I was literally giving up on life, but I heard a voice speak to me instantly saying, "Purpose cannot die". I thought carefully on the voice, paused for a moment, and said to myself, "this is not my time". I could feel myself giving up. The pain was shocking and unpleasant. It was horrible in my abdomen. The test results from the doctor showed that I had cysts on my ovaries. I could hear myself groaning in excruciating pain. The agonizing screams made it worse, but I could not help it. The pain was extremely bad. My first reaction was to give up but my church was in serious prayer; my husband was in prayer; my children were in prayer.

The doctors were considering the possibility of surgery. Lying on that hospital bed, I started to develop the faith in God that I needed to pull through this illness. Fear and timidity tried to take over my body, but I was determined to fight the fight of faith, knowing the battle belonged to the Lord. I was confident that God would heal me, and I was desperate, so I humbled myself unto the Lord. Isaiah 53:5 reminded me, "… he was wounded for our transgressions, he was bruised for our iniquities: the chastisement of our peace was upon him; and with his stripes we are healed."

The various pain medications they gave me in the hospital were not working. I began to scream profusely between the pain and catching my breaths; but God sent a nurse to encourage me through my pain. She told me that God would come through for me if I just exercise faith in Him because the doctors had already done their best. I pondered on these words. It turned out that this nurse was a Christian.

God indeed came through for me in the hospital. I witnessed many die, even from less serious illnesses than I was facing. God kept me and I was released on medication. Although the devil meant to use this to drive fear into my life and to let me doubt God, my sickness was no mistake. It was to draw me closer to God. No one desires sickness and this is a fact. We may feel helpless, but we must rest on the Lord Jesus Christ. At the time that you really need a Saviour, when you least expect it, God stretches out His healing hand and rescues you. Within two weeks of my release from the hospital, the cysts on my ovaries dried up. God healed me. Subsequent tests revealed that the doctors could not even find a trace of this thing that once plagued me.

I was on the edge of giving up, not able to withstand the pressures of life, but God saw my purpose in Him. One thing I know of the Lord is this–whenever you call on Him with a true heart, He is there to deliver you. The Bible says, "… call upon me in the day of trouble: I will deliver thee, and thou shalt glorify me" (Psalm 50:15). Deliverance will come through God's power.

Psalm 103:1-3 declares, "Bless the Lord, O my soul: and all that is within me, bless his holy name. Bless the Lord, O my soul, and forget not all his benefits: Who forgiveth all thine iniquities; who healeth all thy diseases." How many of us when we are going through terrible sicknesses, tell God that if He heals us, we promise to serve Him until we die? In many cases, we forget what we asked God for, and instead fall back into the same place where we started. In our affliction, we sincerely talked to God with desperation, but we failed to follow His path.

The Prophet Jeremiah asked God to "Heal me, O Lord, and I shall be healed; save me, and I shall be saved: for thou art my praise." (Jer.17:14). If you have ever been in this position, you must know this–there comes a point when we have to make ourselves available for Him not only in our sickness, but also in our faithful and glorious times. Truth be told, there were moments when I felt that God was not doing enough for me; but if I were to depend on feelings alone then that would not make me much of a Christian because the Bible is quick to tell us that our feelings cannot be trusted (Prov.3:5). We ought to live by faith in God and in obedience to His Word. This is our source and foundation. Live in it, not your feelings.

Jesus carried the cross and it was not easy for Him to bear but He did it anyway. Going through my sickness was not easy, but I grew through it. I learned the importance of praying fervently, praying devotedly. Moreover, I believe the more you pray the more your prayer becomes effective. Nothing beats the power of prayer. It is a lifestyle, one that we cannot do without.

One of the most important ingredients for answered prayer is faith. Mark 11:23 tells us, "For verily I say unto you, that whosoever shall say unto this mountain be thou removed and be thou cast into the sea and, shall not doubt in his heart but shall believe that those things which he saith shall come to pass he shall have whatsoever he saith."

During my many years of sickness, I learned to build my faith, but the more I climbed in my faith is the more I found myself fighting a battle. I began asking myself, how can I do the work of God and keep on fighting battles? The deeper I went in the Lord, the more it felt like I was fighting a war. Every time I grew higher, I became a target to the devil, but I turned it over to the Lord. As a soldier for God, I knew I needed my spiritual sword, for without it I cannot approach my attacker. Through my sickness, God's empowerment allowed me to exercise my faith to face the storm.

I began to water my faith with the Word of God. It is written in Hebrews 11:1 that, "faith is the substance of things hoped for, the evidence of things not seen." I started to forget about my sickness and stopped casting blame on God. I held close to my heart the words of Paul in Romans 8:38-39, "For I am persuaded that neither death, nor life, nor angels, nor principalities, nor powers, nor things present, nor things to come, nor height, nor depth, nor any other creature, shall be able to separate us from the love of God, which is in Christ Jesus our Lord."

I once read the Bible occasionally, but now I cannot seem to get enough. It has made dramatic changes in my life. In fact, God gave me the written Word to prepare me to live out my faith. What I especially love about God's Word is how it describes itself in different ways. It calls itself a hammer, a sword and a scalpel–all of those are tools designed to make radical changes. God's truth is also described as water, milk, bread, and meat. What do all these things have in common? Well, if you do not eat, drink or take in their nutrients regularly your health will be compromised. It is likewise with

God's Word; we were never meant to live without it. The Bible is essential because it gives me life.

During my sickness, I built a relationship with God. I knew without a doubt He would never leave me nor forsake me. The unchangeable God stood by me until I recovered from my wounds. Many still do not believe that the Redeemer, the efficient One is still in the healing business; but I have a testimony that I have been healed. His work in my life is well accomplished.

Supernatural Healing

In the year 2000 when my son was only three years old, what we thought would be a routine doctor's visit turned out to be one of the worst periods in my life. I took him with me for my doctor's appointment at the hospital. We were in the waiting area, and being the active child that he was, he started to play by running up and down the hall. Unfortunately, he suffered a minimal fall, but there were no noticeable injuries and he looked fine. After my doctor's appointment, we were en route back home in a taxi when suddenly my son started twitching in my hands with seizure-like intensity all over his body. I alerted the driver and he immediately spun around to the hospital's Accident & Emergency Unit. I had called my husband, who was working at the hospital at that time, and relayed what happened. He suggested meeting us at the Emergency Unit. At the ER, our son was roasting with fever and was vomiting. We went to the doctor and explained the situation, but they were curious about what was happening and decided to admit him. My son was hospitalized for ten days.

Everything became tense again. While on the paediatric ward, they ran all possible tests and still could not confirm what was wrong. The doctors then told us that they needed to do one more test because they suspected that he was suffering from meningitis, an inflammation of the membranes that surround the brain and the spinal cord. They explained that they would do a *Lumbar puncture* (Spinal tap) test, where my son would be placed into an "arch" position, and a special needle used to puncture his lower back into the spinal cord. A small amount of cerebral spinal fluid or 'CSF' would be removed and sent for testing to determine if there was an infection. They were extremely careful to tell us the risks associated with this type of test. Some of them include headache, pain or numbness, bleeding and even paralysis. The doctors tried to assure us that they would be extremely cautious in carrying out this procedure. Can you imagine a 3-year-old child enduring this ordeal? Can you imagine how a parent would feel when the possibility exists that their child would be pre-disposed to all those risk factors, and worse may never walk again or even die?

Once again, my faith was being tried and tested. I lifted my voice to God and wept. I decided to challenge fear with faith. I said, "devil! You are a liar and I stand in authority to overcome the torpedo that comes my way." This felt like it was a setback, but I knew God was preparing me for a

The Reality of My Healing

comeback. The Word of God says be strong and courageous (Deut. 31:6); the Lord God charged me to stand and that is exactly what I did. I was not afraid so I stood firm waiting for my son's healing. Nevertheless, the tears were flowing down my face and the hurt was buried inside of me. I began to talk to God, reminding Him of my commitment. "I have fasted, I have prayed, and I am progressing in my walk with You Lord. What am I missing?" Despite my questions, I already declared healing upon his life. I knew the God that I served, and believed that He could do the impossible. I remained calm and sheltered in the Lord, waiting for Him to do the mysterious work on my son's life. My assurance rested on God the healer who is incredible in all His works. He did it already and I knew He could do it again. Faith without works is dead (James 2:26), so I worked with faith to bring God's work to fulfillment.

2 Corinthian 5:7 reminds us, "For we walk by faith and not by sight", and James 1:3 says, "the trying of your faith worketh patience". When you stand in faith, you will endure to the end. With prayer and fasting as my daily bread, I encouraged myself in the Lord and awaited my son's healing. I believed in a good report. Moreover, when it comes to God's works, I do not have to ask how He is going to do it, if He can do it or when He is going to do it, He is Jehovah-Shammah, "the Lord is there." (Ezekiel 48:35). There was no doubt in my mind that my son would be healed. In fact, I believed it before it happened, and on the tenth day he was released from the hospital with no trace of meningitis. His fever and the

twitching were completely gone. The Almighty God completed His job. The God of Jacob proved He was my refuge and strength (Psalm 46:1).

I am touched by the way God changed things in my life. He established His love toward me and my intention is to keep that relationship constantly going. The Bible tells us of the wonderful work He has done. Healing was one of Christ's great missions on the earth. Many saw it and believed, and many still did not believe even after they saw it happen with their own eyes. It is a wonder to know that this continues today; many see the significant works of God and still have not believed, but I can say with surety that Christ did it for me and He did it for my son too. The woman with the issue of blood suffered twelve years and she was healed (St. Mark 5:25 34). Jesus walked on Earth in humanity and healed many people. In St. John 5:5-9, Jesus did one of His miracles at Bethesda where He healed the lame man who was sitting at the pool for 38 years. It was only when Jesus showed up that he received his healing. His work is exceedingly powerful. Friends, God is able, God can, and God will do it for you, if you only believe (Mark 9:23).

The Bible says in Romans 10: 17 that, "Faith cometh by hearing and hearing by the Word of God." I had placed my faith in the power of God's Word to heal my son. You too can do the same. The Bible encourages us to be "doers of the word, and not hearers only" (James 1:22). God gave us the Bible to transform us, not simply to inform us, but to give us peace of mind. The Bible does more than show us what is wrong in our lives. It also tells us how we should live. It radically transforms our lives. With transformation comes application. You need to know how the Word of God applies to you. More than reading the Word, we should also be studying it, memorizing it, meditating on it, and absorbing it.

The Word of God never changes; it is from everlasting to everlasting (Psalm 119:89). It can never become less truthful and will always be exactly what it is from the beginning. This is the advantage of being a Christian; you must accept the truth in the Word concerning your position with Christ. You must accept the truth of being washed clean from your sins and receive a clean conscience because of what has been done for you. This is important because you are able to stand against the lies of Satan when he tries to remind you of your past failures. He will say, "You aren't worthy to receive those promises" but let your faith in the Lord console you. God says in Malachi 4:2, "But unto you that fear my name shall the Sun of righteousness arise with healing in his wings; and ye shall go forth, and grow up as calves of the stall." God will be sure to fulfill His word.

Chapter 4

Hurricane Katrina

In 2005, what I thought would be a normal working year for me in the United States, turned out to be the genesis of a series of illnesses for me, if not a life-changer. As Jamaicans, my colleagues and I were so elated to secure employment in the US, to seek betterment for our families and ourselves. This was because of the farm work and hotel programme partnership agreement between the governments of the United States and Jamaica. This was my fourth time working in the US and my second time in the city of Biloxi, Mississippi. It was just six months into my contract with one of the largest hotels on the Gulf Coast, when the threat of the most devastating hurricane that I have experienced became a reality. On August 29, 2005, I was in Biloxi, Mississippi when Hurricane Katrina obliterated the Gulf Coast. Biloxi is the largest city there, and home to a number of gigantic casino barges. When Katrina struck, all the barges were floated into the city and were left sitting over slabs and in some cases, right over the coastal road of Highway 90. It was a remarkable sight when these humongous casino barges in the middle of what used to be residential areas, all washed ashore. Katrina's wind and storm surge decimated the area that I was residing in, and was responsible for many deaths and billions of dollars in damages.

The area suffered massive damage from the impact, leaving hundreds dead and many missing. I remember at the time being grossly perplexed to see how the homes along the coast were flooded with water. Had it not been for the grace of the Almighty God then I would not be alive today to tell my story. All the Jamaicans on the work programme in that area were evacuated to one shelter. I can vividly recall during the storm, that the floodwaters came within approximately 10 meters from where we were staying at the shelter. The residential houses in and around the shelter were all damaged. I was marooned in, with no possibility of getting out from where I was. In the aftermath of the hurricane, I could see trees blocking every entrance; roads were severely damaged and impassable. Even the cemeteries had given up their dead; bodies were floating all around, miles from where they were initially buried. There was no food and potable water. I did not know what to do or how I would survive. All communication was lost and there was no possible way to contact my husband back home in Jamaica. I knew that he and the rest of my family were worried about me.

It was two days prior to Katrina when we last spoke and I could recall hearing the trepidation in his voice. My only hope was to depend on the Almighty God who kept me through the storm. I was physically and emotionally devastated, traumatized, and distressed. The onset of dehydration was now affecting me. It had been two days in the aftermath, without food and drinking water. I became sick in body and emotionally disturbed. I asked myself the question, "what must I do?" I asked God why He would take me into a foreign country just to let me die. With tears running down my face and on the verge of giving up, I heard the Lord remind me of Isaiah 43:2 (NIV) "When you pass through the waters, I will be with you; and when you pass through the rivers, they will not sweep over you. When you walk through the fire, you will not be burned; the flames will not set you ablaze." On the third day, God proved Himself my Jehovah-Jireh– "The Lord will provide" (Gen. 22:14). Like Elijah and the widow of Zarephath (I Kings 17:7-16), He divinely orchestrated a nearby Walmart to provide food and water until the Jamaican government made preparation to fly us out of the country. The eternal God enabled me to "ride out my storm." My hope in the Lord was restored. God gave me a new lease on life. On September 5, 2005, I was safely back in the comfort of my own home in Jamaica. God's protection was with me. Had it not been for the Lord on my side where would I be? I was shattered, but I found refuge in the shadow of His wings (Psalm 57:1).

Even though I survived Hurricane Katrina, the remnant of her was still lingering with me. This deadly storm caused me much suffering mentally, emotionally and ultimately physically. I had horrible nightmares, suffered from sleepless nights, and experienced a loss in appetite. Between the months of September to December 2005, I went through a series of visitations to doctors and was the subject of various tests. It appeared as if there was no relief for me. I was having very frequent and irregular headaches and had lost a lot of weight so much so that people were saying I had either cancer or diabetes. Some were even encouraging me to go to "other sources" to find out what was really happening to me. All those pronouncements just caused me to be fearful even more, and I lost sight of what God had in store for me. The life-transforming events of Katrina led to the beginning of the biggest illness that I had gone through–a brain tumour, called *meningioma*.

Bleeding in the Brain: Part 1

2005 had been a devastating year for me. It marked the onset of my illnesses, and I found out that I was bleeding from the brain. What would be a normal hospital visit turned out to be a dreadful experience. On the morning of December 11, 2005 I went to the University Hospital of the West Indies (UHWI) for an unusual headache that I was having. After consultation with the doctor, he informed me that I was experiencing a migraine headache and as a result prescribed a medication that would help ease the pain. Little did I know that this medication could have cost me my life.

In the wee hours of the morning that day, I was awakened

by a terrible pain in my head. It felt like someone was beating me in the back of my head with a hammer. I could hardly stand; the pain was so severe that when I screamed it seemed like my head was splitting in two. I could hardly see; my neck and entire body was in pain. I could not pray and it was the last thing on my mind. In all honesty, I really just needed to find some solution to ease the pain. It was excruciating and nothing could have stopped it. I screamed, called on the name of Jesus but nothing could stop this pain. On one occasion, I got up off the bed to go to the bathroom. On my way there, my eyes went dim; I could not see anything. I screamed for my husband, who rushed to my assistance just in time before I passed out in his hands.

He rushed me to the emergency room at the University Hospital of the West Indies (UHWI) where a CT scan was done on my brain. The results showed that I was bleeding from the back of my brain and there was a clot. In the doctors' assessment, they concluded that the medication prescribed the day before caused the bleeding. They explained that due to its strength, it contracted and ruptured the blood vessels in my head. This resulted in a life-threatening type of stroke caused by bleeding into the space surrounding the brain. I was admitted to the hospital in serious condition.

On the ward, I was placed on bed number three. That same night, the patient on bed number one died. There was tension all around. Not long after that the patient on bed number two also died. By this time, I was ready to say my final goodbyes. My husband was there with me and tried to console me. Instead of his usual macho temperament, I could see his vulnerability. Nothing he said or did worked. Like me, he was nervous and seemingly broken. I waited anxiously, wondering if this was it. "God, is this my time?" Unbelievably, the patient on bed number four died about three hours after. I was in shock and was so emotionally disturbed. This was a bitter-sweet moment for me–bitter, because of all those deaths in one night, but sweet because the Lord was gracious to spare me. The death angel had skipped me. It was as if God was telling me what He told Moses and Aaron in Exodus 12:13, "...when I see the blood, I will pass over you, and the plague shall not be upon you to destroy you..." This incredible God stopped by and decided to save my life. Isn't that awesome? The Prophet Jeremiah reminded me in Lamentations 3:22-23 that, "The steadfast love of the Lord never ceases; his mercies never come to an end; they are new every morning; great is your faithfulness." Once more, I had experienced the bountiful love of God. The magnificent One gave me another chance. Who could it be but Jesus Christ? As Scripture records, "For all power belongs to God, now and forever." (1 Peter 5:11 NIV). It was sheer rejoicing when my husband returned to the ward the following morning and saw that I was still alive.

Our gladness was short-lived however because the pain became worse. This time I could neither walk, nor sit, nor eat. The doctor ran some more tests and the results showed that I was suffering from a rare type of migraine known as *Basilar Migraine*, one that begins in the brain stem. He explained that its cause is unknown but may be the result of a tightening blood vessel. When this becomes too tight, it blocks blood flow.

I was under strict observations and regulations as the doctors and nurses feared that I could have a seizure or stroke anytime. As a precaution, they even raised the side rails of the bed to prevent rolling or a fall in the event of convulsion. Like a prisoner, I was on lock-down. Visitations were restricted to my immediate family only, and for two days, I was under heavy scrutiny. In all of that, I had been praying without ceasing and this time I experienced a miraculous breakthrough.

The next morning, I was able to walk to the bathroom by myself. I know it is unbelievable but I walked back to my bed without hindrance or assistance. I knew how I felt within my body and it was very different. It was breathtaking to see myself moving all around again. Eventually, the bleeding stopped. This puzzled doctors who asked amongst themselves, "What happened?" "Where did the blood go? and "where did the clot move to?" This appeared questionable to these medical practitioners, but whose report do we believe? I know I believed the report of the Lord. Doctors were searching for answers because the blood was not in the brain neither had it moved to any part of the body. I was feeling quite normal, the pain was gone, the blood was no more in the brain, and the clot was unseen. This puzzled the doctors but not the King of all kings. His work was made complete without doctors and nurses because He is the greatest physician.

In 1 Samuel 2:6 Hannah praises God saying, "The Lord

killeth and maketh alive; he bringeth down to the grave and bringeth up." The doctors said it was impressive to see that I had recovered without doing an operation. A miraculous work was done in my life. The next day, I was released from the hospital. I knew it was my faith that kept me going. I fought with all my might, with the Heavenly Father on my side. The Bible says in 1 John 4:4 "Ye are of God, little children, and have overcome them: for greater is He that is in you, than he that is in the world." Once again, I was victorious through Jesus Christ.

On a subsequent visit to the hospital's clinic, the resident doctor was so surprised to see me and asked, "Are you still alive?" I was stunned by that question, but I knew that the God who made me transformed me. He rebuilt and renewed me. I was not a surprise to Him, so I did not feel discouraged by what the doctor asked. I did not have to contemplate if God was with me; I knew that He was. Furthermore, what was complicated to the physician was not complicated to God because He knows how to correct every wrong move.

God knows *the end* from *the beginning* (Isaiah 46:10). What the doctors might not have known was that when God heals, He transforms and rebuilds you for His purpose. The doctors may have put their faith in their medical expertise, but I have learned to put my faith in God. Everything around us is sinking and failing except the Word of Almighty God. He desires for men to build their faith in Him, and to believe Him. Scripture records at least three instances after Jesus performed healing He said, *"Thy faith hath made thee whole"*

(Mark 5:34; Mark 10:52 & Luke 17:19, emphasis added) Faith is a powerful key that unlocks miraculous healing.

Healing was one of Jesus' greatest ministries on earth. He did it then and He is still doing it now. He reassures us that His healing power never changes. God allows us to call on Him when we are weak and broken. He knows, He sees, and He feels. His compassion never changes. As believers, we still have this hope and assurance that our God is able to do impossible things. Sometimes we waiver about our healing, believing it will happen instantly because we know He is God. We have to wait on Him. Those that wait on the Lord shall renew their strength (Isaiah 40:31). We read and study His Word, but when the forces of darkness have been unleashed upon us, we tend to become weary. Do not give up! Like Moses in Exodus 17:11, our hands may become weary sometimes and our strength may fail, but God will send both Aaron and Hur to uphold us.

Many Christians lost the fight of faith because they refused to wait on God. They gave up, even sometimes at the point of their breakthrough. Did you know that the hardest part between seedtime and harvest, between sowing and reaping, is the waiting period? Wait on the Lord be of good courage and he will strengthen thine heart (Psalm 27:14). As a survivor, I've learned never to leave the Word of God because it is a tool that can deliver you from danger by strengthening your faith. In Hebrew 11:6, we are told that "without faith it is impossible to please God". Our Lord wants a firm believer who stands in faith and fights.

ANOTHER BLEEDING IN THE BRAIN

Approaching the anniversary of the first bleeding in the brain in 2005, was another bleeding in the brain in December 2006. I had just completed my daily chores and reclined to take a rest when suddenly, I could hardly see and there was little mobility on my right side – I could not move my right hand, not even to clench my fist. Once again, my husband rushed me to the Accident & Emergency Unit at the University Hospital of the West Indies where I was carried by stretcher into the Radiology Unit to do a Magnetic Resonance Angiography (MRA) with contrast of my brain.

An IV catheter was placed in my arm and a contrast agent injected into it. This is part of a procedure that allows the radiologist to distinguish normal from abnormal conditions in the body. After the scans were examined by the doctors, they determined that the bleeding occurred in another part of the brain and not in the same area as the first one. They were all astonished to know that I was still alive. The consultant neurologist exclaimed that bleeding in the brain once was too many, but twice was a first for him in all his years of practicing medicine. By this I knew that the hand of the Lord was upon me. Once again, I was admitted to the ward. I could hear some of the nurses who were there in 2005 screaming in disbelief.

Eleven years into my Christian walk and here I was again, lying on a hospital bed writhing in pain. It was in full force. I was walking, sleeping and eating in pain. I hardly slept and the numerous times that I was given the painkillers almost turned me into a drug addict, yet they could not help. My mind was traumatized. This pain was destroying my life completely and the only word I knew to say was "JESUS!" I could not pray, could not talk to Him, but I could call Him by His name, "JESUS!"

There were many sleepless nights. Only my husband could tell someone the kind of pain that I was feeling. He was right there with me, praying me through. He fasted and prayed but there were no immediate answers to my problem. Doctors could not help. Bleeding in the brain was my cross. I struggled with pain but I carried my cross. I could hardly walk but I still carried my cross, knowing that Jehovah Rapha, the Lord who heals (Ex.15:26), He never made any mistakes when He healed me.

Unless you have experienced God's move in your life

physically and spiritually, you may not understand the magnitude of His power. Have you ever felt like your life was slowly slipping from you? Have you felt God move mysteriously in your pain, especially in the middle of the night? Have your tears overflowed like a well? What do you do when you want to walk but cannot move unless someone moves you? You cannot sit because of pain, cannot sleep, cannot pray and the only person you see beside you praying is your husband? Where do you find strength when you have no words to say to the Lord and groaning in the Spirit is the only thing you can do? What will you do at three o' clock in the morning when you are confused because pain has affected you mentally, physically, and spiritually? The Holy Spirit Himself interceded for me constantly, until Jehovah Rapha, the affectionate, compassionate healer stopped by.

Unlike the first episode, this time I constantly called on the name of Jesus. The doctors and nurses could not understand why I kept on calling on that Name. Some were even wondering if I had gone crazy, and whether to call the psychiatrist. I had done a CT scan and an MRI, but God was on my side; my brain was not swelling and the blood had dried up. After two weeks, I was pain free and showed signs of improvement. My mobility returned and there was strength all over my body. The doctors took the decision to release me that Sunday night, December 31, 2006.

I know you may be tempted to ask the question, why didn't God just clear all that bleeding at once? I do not have the answer because the Lord tells us that His ways are "past finding out" (Romans 11:33), and that His thoughts are higher than our thoughts (Isaiah 55:8-9). The answer lies with God. Isaiah 41:10 reminds us, "fear thou not; for I am with thee: be not dismayed; for I am thy God: I will strengthen thee I will help thee; yea I will uphold thee with the right hand of my righteousness." Moreover, Luke 1:37 tells me "for with God nothing shall be impossible."

As a believer, I humbled myself throughout the pain. God spoke in His Word in Matthew 19:26, "...with men this is impossible but with God all things are possible." In all that pain, I realized that I still had my Saviour right there beside me. Sometimes throughout my sickness I wanted to give up, because when you are in pain the world is black before you. You're blind to everything; but one thing I know is the name of Jesus and it is through His name and blood that I was healed. Doctors believed that I was not going to live, but God who is infinite performed an incomprehensible work in my life, leaving friends and family and medical professionals astonished at the miraculous work in me.

I am a walking testimony and my faith is real. It is not easy to battle sickness, but I have learned to take comfort in the God who is Lord over all sicknesses and diseases. There is great power when you call on the name of Jesus in faith. When we say it, it tells who we are; it is what we are known by to all those around us. There is nothing more powerful than the name Jesus. Sickness has to flee when we call upon the name of Jesus. The Bible says, "The name of the Lord is a strong tower: the righteous runneth into it and is safe."

(Proverb 18:10). In a world that often feels chaotic and fearful, His name is the one to hold close. If you call on Him, He will answer you (Jer. 33:3).

Many people believe that your mind is the healer, but that is not so. God is the source of all healing (Psalm 103:3). His healing power is immeasurable. Even when healing takes place through the work of a physician, God is behind it all. In Matthew 10:8 Jesus commanded the twelve to go heal the sick, cleanse the lepers, raise the dead and cast out devils. Think about it! How could Jesus entrust His disciples to do those things? The answer is straightforward–He has the power and authority to do so (1 Peter 3:22), and He is the source of all that is good and perfect (James 1:17).

Some questions many have asked are, "Can God do these things the Bible says He will do? Can He do it in our time?" or "If He is the Healer why can't God prevent us from sickness?" The Bible is clear in its position when it says, "is any sick among you? let him call for the elders of the church; and let them pray over him anointing him with oil in the name of the Lord: and the prayer of faith shall save the sick, and the Lord shall raise him up; and if he have committed sins, they shall be forgiven him" (James 5:14-15). I am a living testimony that God can heal you and turn your life around so that you are able to serve Him faithfully. All God needs for us is to serve Him in spirit and in truth.

On my way from the hospital that Sunday night on December 31, 2006, I went straight to my then local church to share with the brethren in our annual *'Watch night'* service.

I could not keep silent; I had to give birth to that which the Lord had placed within me. I had to testify about the goodness of God and how he raised me up because purpose was on my life. The Bible tells us in Revelation 12:11 "And they overcame him by the blood of the Lamb and by the word of their testimony..." My testimony resulted in some souls being saved for the Kingdom.

Another Tragedy Strikes

Since I accepted Jesus Christ as my personal Saviour, I've asked the question, why has God allowed misfortune in my life? After going through my battle and pain in 2006, I thought all sickness, hurt and disappointments were over. This was not quite the case. In 2007, tragedy struck once more. My father died from a stroke, leaving me to again ask the question, "why?" These trials were a thorn in my flesh. I was unstable and crushed inside, but in this storm, I remembered that God was still gracious and kind. I asked myself the question, "how can I displease God after everything He had done in my life?" Instantly, I asked Him to journey with me through this one. With tears flowing from my eyes, I cried aloud saying, "I can't do it alone, walk with me Lord."

God did not heal my father, but chose to take him home. It was a devastating and stressful time, but God was taking me through it. When faced with the difficulties of life, people often ask, "Where is God?" and "Why won't God help me?" or "When is God going to help me?", "Is God hearing me?

The Reality of My Healing

"Is God dead or is He alive? In these rough times, I remind myself that God is supreme. He sees what we do not or cannot see. He knows what we do not know and He works accordingly as He wills.

Many people hate God because their loved ones died, or have an incurable illness. They are in earnest prayer and cannot get any answer. I know that such seasons are bitter, but we ought to remember that, "It is appointed unto man once to die" (Hebrew 9:27). At the same time, we can find hope knowing that Christ has already borne our grief and our pain. He has promised to wipe away our tears according to Revelation 21:4, "And God shall wipe away all tears from their eyes and there shall be no more death, neither sorrow, nor crying neither there shall be no more pain for the former things are passed away."

After my father's passing, Christ gave my family and I comfort in every way. What manner of man is He that gave His life for me? We ignored Him and we denied Him, but grace did it for us. I was paralyzed with fear, but because of God's intervention in my life, I became wiser and smarter for God.

Chapter 6

THE MYSTERY HEALING: BRAIN TUMOUR

In 2007, as the New Year begun, doctors ordered that I enroll in the Neuro-surgery clinic of the hospital and begin annual MRI check-ups. I attended all the scheduled clinics and MRI screenings. I knew that God was working in my life to bring about complete healing, but wisdom also dictated that I follow the doctors' orders. All the tests performed during those times revealed that there was neither swelling nor bleeding in my brain. It was great news, but little did I know that, the battle was not yet over. The doctors had given me clearance to work, so in 2008 I returned to the United States.

One night in October 2009, I came from a long and rough day at work. I was sitting quietly in the living hall, having a long-distance telephone conversation with my husband who was in Jamaica. While talking to him, I felt a sudden pain on the right side of my neck rushing straight down to my spine. I screamed loudly. My husband started to panic because he was not hearing anything from me. I was on the floor, unconscious and unable to move. My fellow co-workers rushed me to the Emergency Room at the University of New Orleans Medical hospital. By this time, I had regained consciousness. Several doctors in the ER quickly attended to me. Though conscious, I was unable to walk. They ordered me to do some tests because of my brain's medical history.

When the results came back, there was bleeding again; this time with a twist–a tumour was present. One of the doctors shouted, "she has cancer." Once again, I was gripped with fear and the looks on my co-workers' faces were dismal. Doctors began moving quickly to stop the bleeding. At the same time, I was having a seizure and stroke. Nevertheless, I was conscious. The doctors could not believe that I was still alive. I was placed under the MRI machine more than once to see what really happened. More tests were done all over my body, including my heart–four hundred and fifty scans, from head to toe. The blood stopped eventually, but doctors still wanted to find out where it went. They could not find any evidence in the body to prove that it was lodged elsewhere. After running a series of tests, the doctors ordered another ultrasound on my heart. When the results returned normal, they decided to place me under the MRI machine again because they still did not understand why so much damage occurred, and the blood was gone without a trace. I remained calm in the midst of it all because I knew the God I served.

Doctors struggled to understand the miracle behind the bleeding. The name of the tumour was *meningioma*. I learned that it may compress or squeeze the adjacent brain, nerves, and vessels and can result in serious disability or death. It measured 2cm and was located on the right side of my brain. The doctors explained that due to the size of the tumour and its location, surgery was not an option because it was too small and may be impossible to find. Doctors were still searching! "Where did the blood go?" they asked, trying to figure out the supernatural thing that happened. "How could one person bleed on the brain three times and still be alive?" screamed the nurses. They were all astonished having seen the scar tissues from the prior bleedings and the newly discovered tumour, yet there was minimal damage to the brain and no trace of the blood. The MRI showed where the damage occurred, but there was not one drop of blood left at the spot. How, why and what happened? Only God has the answer. This was another miraculous healing by the Heavenly Father.

After a week in this new hospital facility, my seizure and stroke were gone. The test result was remarkable. I was sent home. When I followed up on my MRI result, it showed that the tumour was gradually shrinking. My body functions had returned to normal. The doctors recommended that my best course of treatment was to remain on medication, to prevent seizures and to alleviate the pain. It has been ten years since I was set free from my brain condition. I do not have to ask anyone who I am. I know God created me for a purpose, and that purpose is to serve Him.

Maybe you are going through a similar situation and feel scared that the disease affecting you is incurable. Remember this–there is another part to your sickness, the answer is healing from God. He has done it repeatedly for many persons like me and He will do the same for you. This is the reality of my healing. He is capable of handling everything in His own way, because He is sovereign. Christ understands our problems. He has experienced our pain, heartache, and distress. In His humanity, He experienced all the agony while He was on earth. He suffered just as we suffer today. Do not give up, fight with all your might! Ask God for strength and energy. No matter how your body feels or looks, God can still do a miracle in your life. No other authority is above His. He has a listening ear to act and will answer when you cry out to Him. Sometime our sickness is consistent and it seems like there is no way out, but remember He promises that He will never leave us nor forsake us (Deut. 31:6; Heb. 13:5).

Perseverance through Bible College

In late 2011 while still working in the United States, the Lord impressed upon my heart to attend Bible college back home in Jamaica. I did not take it seriously and almost rubbished the thought at the time. I thought that I needed to work to supplement my husband's income, and to provide funding for my daughter who was enrolled at university. However, like Jesus said to Saul (later Paul) on the Damascus road in Acts 9:5, it is "hard to kick against the prick." No one can oppose God and win. I tried to reason out all the possibilities why I should not attend, but I was being disobedient. God said in His Word, "To obey is better than sacrifice" (1 Sam. 15:22). I heeded God's call.

I began Bible college in January 2012, pursuing a programme in Biblical and Pastoral Studies. I entered at the start of the second semester. The Lord won again! There I was in 2011 with no desire to go, but I was now enrolled, entering another sphere of my life. I had forsaken all and heeded the call of God. I believed Bible college was where I tested and proved God. It was a test of patience and resilience. It also tested my knowledge because I had been out of the formal educational system for over twelve years. It challenged my financial resources too.

In my first year, I struggled with financial problems and other difficulties, such as the volume of class work, assignments, and course load. However, did you know that impossible circumstances allow God's glory to shine brightest? God pulled me through my first year without fail.

During my second year, I was stricken with another ailment. This time it was my heart. I was having frequent palpitations so much so that I had to visit the doctor to find out the cause. After several electrocardiograms (ECGs), and wearing a forty-eight-hour holter monitor on my chest along with X-rays and numerous blood tests, there was no indication of what was wrong. The doctors took another step. They inserted an implantable loop recorder on the right side of my chest to monitor and record the rhythm of my heart. I wore it for three months.

After the three months elapsed, the heart specialist called me in to check on the device. Finally, the loop recorder was the one that captured the problem in the rhythm of my heart. Many specialists said that this was a very difficult problem to identify. On this visit, I was told that my heart's rhythm was becoming extremely irregular and I needed to get to the hospital within twenty-four hours for surgery. The specialist explained that without surgery, I had at most six months to live. My body was in total shock knowing that death was right at my doorsteps and I could do nothing about it. I could neither run nor hide, and I could not find words to pray nor remember any Bible verses to quote. I was completely out of it. Imagine the same God that healed me from stroke, seizures, and bleeding in the brain would call me to Bible college just to let me die? The devil is a liar! He cannot thwart God's purpose; at best, he can only disrupt it. Job 42:2 (NIV) affirms this, "I know that you can do all things; no purpose of yours can be thwarted."

I was now in a race against time. The device needed to save my life was very expensive and I also understood that many patients with similar conditions died because they could not afford it; likewise, many also died before they could finish paying for it. However, the Lord had been faithful in His promises to supply all my need, according to His riches in glory by Christ Jesus (Philippians 4:19). The Lord looked ahead in time, and years before, He strategically placed my husband in a job at the same hospital that I had been receiving treatment. He foreknew that those times would come.

When my husband contacted the manager of the new Surgical Intensive Care Unit, she informed him that only one device remained, and to procure another from the vendor in the United States would take at least four to six weeks. By this time, my husband and I were in a quandary. Where would we get the money to buy it, and what if someone else bought it first? We prayed earnestly and the Lord immediately changed the situation. He began to send financial help from my local church and the Bible college. The insurance company covered some of the costs and the remaining balance came directly from our own funds.

Restoring the Rhythm of Life

I allowed the Holy Spirit of God to work through me and build my faith during the operation. The doctors took the decision to place an Implantable Cardioverter Defibrillator (ICD) inside my heart. This was necessary because I used to suffer from rapid and irregular heartbeat. Sometimes my heart used to beat too quickly and as explained by the doctors, the impulses started in the lower chambers; so I had what is called *Ventricular Tachycardia* (VT). This means that whenever my heart went into VT, it may not pump blood as efficiently as it does during a normal rhythm. Rapid contractions prevented it from filling adequately with blood between beats.

Less blood would reach my brain and sometimes that made my heart pound, or I felt faint or dizzy and even passed out.

After being carried into the Operating Room, I was reminded of what God said in Joshua 1:9, "Have not I commanded thee? Be strong and of a good courage; be not afraid, neither be thou dismayed: for the Lord thy God is with thee whithersoever thou goest." With fear in my eyes, I began to sing my way to sleep, leaving everything to the Almighty and the heart specialist whom the Holy Spirit worked through to complete a wonderful job.

I can recall when the doctors and nurses put me under local anaesthesia. Shortly after, I did not remember anything. After the nearly 4-hour long procedure, the doctors told me that I was dead for 5 minutes. That's right. I was clinically dead. They explained that a small incision, approximately 4 inches, was made in my upper chest where the defibrillator was inserted. They then carefully and precisely guided two leads through the veins into my heart and then connected them to the defibrillator. Here is the scary part–the settings were programmed and it was now time to test that the device was working properly. In order to do this, they had to put me on a life support machine and stop my heart for 5 minutes so that the device could function on its own. I would be shocked back to life again to breathe on my own. Imagine that! What if the device had malfunctioned? Maybe you would be reading my tribute instead of my testimony. Thank God for working behind the scenes and guiding those doctors to successfully perform the procedure. All the leads would have to be working before I could be awakened. I cannot tell you what happened because I was unconscious, but God gave me the answer to share with you all. Each lead represented one of Jesus' stripes for healing and this is why I am alive today. No man can give the breath of life except God. If He did it for me, He can do it for you.

I awoke rejoicing in the Lord for His merciful work done in my life. One thing I am sure of, the Holy Spirit empowered me to overcome my fears. I had recovered from all the darts that the enemy threw at me. The surgery was successful.

After six weeks, I returned to Bible college with a brand-new lease on life. It was as if I did not miss anything. All the notes, assignments and other class materials were already saved by one of my classmates, and I was given time to complete them. God gave me the balance and stability I needed to finish them all and again without failing a single one. The battle intensified when I entered my third and final year. Some of the students who started and ended second year with me did not return for various reasons. This was it! Third year was where the rubber met the road, where we had to put the pedal to the metal. There were stress factors such as numerous assignments and presentations, preparation and delivery of sermons, the chapel sessions where we preached, rallies, and visitations to other churches. All these and more were required. At the same time, I was trying to lead a normal life with a device implanted in me.

Due to the delicate nature of my heart condition, the

principal often asked me if I was able to manage student responsibilities such as preaching or moderating services. I always answered with a resounding "yes" because I had the faith and confidence in God to strengthen and to uphold me. I knew that perseverance was going to be the key. I began to reason with myself, saying that I had to press my way out. I will not come this far to give up now. Finally, I began to talk to God. I told Him to give me patience. I told Him that I would wait diligently for His direction and guidance. I knew that would be a long and painful process, but I would wait. I remembered His Word in I Chronicle 16:11 "Seek the Lord and his strength; seek his presence continually." I held on to a prophetic word that said, "It is well!"(2 Kings 4:26).

I remembered when I was going out on a particular rally with my batch mates and my husband drove me to the location where we should all meet up. While he was reversing the car, one of the wheels ran over my right foot. I was in pain for the entire journey, but when it was time to lead the service, it was gone. I felt no more pain until I was back home. The next day I visited the doctor, had an X-ray done, and thanks be to God there was no fractures or broken bones. It was all God. He knew that I was faithful to Him and He healed me. Throughout Bible college, God was there to strengthen me. He said, "Be strong my daughter." 2 Corinthians 12:9 encouraged me to remain steadfast, "And he said unto me, my grace is sufficient for thee: for my strength is made perfect in weakness. Most gladly therefore will I rather glory in my infirmities that the power of Christ may rest upon me".

In October 2014, after three years of endurance and perseverance, I graduated with a diploma in Biblical and Pastoral Studies. My experience in Bible college had transformed me. Fear diminished, and faith in God developed. I could recall when I was marching up that podium to collect the trophy for *"The most resilient student"* that the Lord reminded me that He has not given me a spirit of fear, but of power and of love and of a sound mind (2 Timothy 1:7). It was as if all the scriptures that I had learned were finally making sense to me when I began to apply them to my life. I declared that I made it and it was all because of the grace and mercy of the Almighty God. I affirmed the words of the Apostle Paul who said, "I press toward the mark for the prize of the high calling of God in Christ Jesus." (Philippians 3:14). My willingness to serve God was part of my dedication because God rebuilt me all over again.

With my faith strengthened, I am now able to stand against Satan when he tries to remind me of my past failures and tell me that I am not worthy to receive God's promises. My faith and perseverance kept me throughout Bible college. I was determined that my faith would produce fruit. I reminded myself of my identity–a strong believer, exercising my faith. Moses was trained to lead God's people out of Egyptian bondage. Similarly, I had to go through the process of training to propel me into the ministry of evangelism. I had been mandated by God to "Go out into the highways and hedges and compel them to come in" (Luke 14:23). God has called and prepared me for "such a time as this" (Esther 4:14).

The Reality of My Healing

It has been five years now since I graduated from Bible college and six years since the ICD was placed above my heart to treat the rhythm disorder. When it was first inserted, the heart specialist said I would experience shock whenever it detects a life-threatening rapid heart rhythm. It would try to slow the rhythm to get it back to normal. Thank God for His tender mercy towards me. These past six years, I have never received a single shock from the device. My heart's rhythms are normal and today I am still leading a full life without fear, but with the added security that my God is still able. It is His grace and mercy that brought me thus far and is keeping me still. God decided to give me another chance.

The reality of my healing was not an accident. The Almighty God clearly orchestrated it. Having a heart condition is something I have to live with for the rest of my life; but the truth of the matter is, with God on my side, I am stronger physically, spiritually and emotionally. My heart is no hindrance to me. I can still do God's work. I can run, skip, jump, and most of all preach the Word of God.

If you are currently facing an illness, know this–you are not helpless; get up, stand up, run your race. Let the enemy know that all power and authority belong to God and He has released it upon you . He said in His Words, "I am the Lord that healeth thee" (Exodus 15:26). Know that even when we fall, feel crushed, and want to give up, God is there to pick up the pieces and put them back together again. God will deliver you from brokenness. Do not get frustrated! Cry aloud! Help is on the way. If you believe that God can heal you, announce

The Mystery Healing: Brain Tumour

His power to that package of sickness that wants to devour your life. Let God destroy every yoke of bondage. Hold on my sister! Hold on my brother! God is here to roll your stone away. There is nothing impossible for God. Exercise your faith and prove Him.

REBUILT FOR MINISTRY: PREACHING AND EVANGELISM

Shortly after Bible school, I followed my calling and moved straight into the ministry of evangelism. God gave me a passion to earnestly take the Word to His people. Jesus tells us in His great commission to "Go and make disciples of all nations" (Matthew 28:19, NIV). Jesus wants people to know exactly how it feels to be touched by Him and to be made whole. He has used me to assure others that healing is a reality and that they too can be delivered by His mighty hand and outstretched arm (Deut. 26:8). With this testimony, many have accepted God as their personal Saviour and have been walking with Him since. He wants people to recognize that He is God and His work is unquestionable. He wants us to teach sinners His truth, whether we take the good news to them publicly or privately.

Before preaching the gospel, I realized my need to become stronger and wiser in the Lord. It is true that if we do not study the Word, we become empty vessels ready to fall. Furthermore, if we do not stand in Him, we are not ready to demonstrate His authority. When we feed on His Word, He will fill our vessels and cause life to flow into us. The Bible says in St. John 6:57, "As the living Father hath sent me, and I live by the Father: so he that eateth me, even he shall live by me."

As an evangelist, I try to bring the Word of God to my family first. My children love God and I am most impressed that my son loves God with all his heart. A day has never passed that he does not ask for prayer. He believes in prayer intensely, and this convinces me that the work of evangelism is effective in my home. I am imploring you to make your home one of prayer.

If you are not saved, ask God to intervene and change it completely. As the Word of God says in 1 Chronicles 16:11, "Seek the Lord and his strength; seek his face continually."

I am sold out to the work that Christ has called me to do. In Luke 14:23 we read of the instruction to "go out into the highways and hedges, and compel them to come in, that my house may be filled." God needs souls for His kingdom and I know whatever it takes, He will strengthen me to minister anywhere in the world. Sharing the gospel to sinners is the heart of evangelism, and every person should have the opportunity to have a relationship with Jesus.

Jesus told His disciples in Acts 1:8 (NIV), "But you will

receive power when the Holy Spirit comes on you; and you will be my witnesses in Jerusalem, and in all Judea and Samaria, and to the ends of the earth." My ministry of evangelism began in my home and community; this was my witness in Jerusalem. I have visited over five parishes across Jamaica to preach; this was my "Judea and Samaria" experience. Most of my preaching takes place in the local church where I also serve as President of the women's ministry. I am entrusted with an awesome responsibility to effect changes in the women I lead. I have also preached at street meetings, open-air meetings, and internal crusades.

I remember the first time that I received an invitation to preach at a church in the parish of St. Thomas, Jamaica. It was my first sermon outside of chapel sessions and rallies in Bible college. I was both fearful and nervous because I did not want to make any mistakes. The thought of preaching to a large audience got me so nervous that I literally shook the pulpit. I used to battle nerves when preaching the Word of God because I wanted everything to be perfect. Like Moses in Exodus 4:10, I thought that I was not eloquent enough to preach and at times would make excuses to shy away from some engagements. Over the last five years of preaching, I have learned to overcome my fear instead of allowing it to cripple me. I am comforted by the Apostle Paul's words in 1 Corinthians 2:3 (NIV), "I came to you in weakness with great fear and trembling." If this great servant of God struggled with nerves, then why should I be so concerned about my ability?

Rebuilt for Ministry: Preaching and Evangelism

Prayer was another method I used to conquer my fear of preaching. I prayed to God earnestly that the power of His Spirit would rest heavily upon me during ministry. I encouraged others to pray for me. Indeed, the Apostle Paul emphasizes this vital element of overcoming fear in Ephesians 6:19 (NIV), "Pray also for me, that whenever I speak, words may be given me so that I will fearlessly make known the mystery of the gospel".

The ministry of evangelism has also led me to the United States to preach and win souls for the kingdom of God, whether I am there for work or vacation. This was my "to the ends of the earth" experience. God has opened up doors and mandated me as a missionary to fulfill His work of soul winning. It does not matter where I am or who you are, I preach the unadulterated and undiluted Word of God with intensity. His presence has afforded me the privilege, power, and unction I need to preach with impact. After all, "He must increase, but I must decrease" (St. John 3:30).

Concluding Thoughts

The moment I realized that God is my reason for living, I began to develop a closer relationship with Him. It was not easy for me to conquer sickness. I could not do it alone. The Almighty God wrapped me tightly and carried me through. The Lord has transformed me for His purpose. The advanced healing in my life showed God to be the most dependable and irreplaceable being than anyone I have ever come across. My healing was not about me, rather, it was about the works of God done in my life so that others may see His glory.

My struggle with fear gave me the persistence to lift my faith and see the instantaneous healing power of God. He ordained me as a promise and called me to ministry. I am evangelizing and winning souls for the Kingdom; it is my joy to do the work of the Lord. As He continues to give me assignments, I am reminded of Isaiah 6:8, "I heard the voice of the Lord saying, Whom shall I send? And who will go for us?" Like Isaiah, my response to the Lord is "Here am I. Send me."

A Special Appeal to Unbelievers

God has a compassionate love for you and desires that you be saved by moving from darkness to light. He wants to transform your life so that His glory shines through. He will work His miracle in your life to show His extraordinary power.

The undisputable God is able to do anything and everything in our lives. The Apostle Paul caught this revelation when he said, "Now unto him that is able to do exceedingly abundantly above all that we ask or think, according to the power that worketh in us" (Eph.3:20).

If you have been through any kind of tragedy, you may have asked the age-old question, "Where is God?" You may have even blamed God for it, but right now, I encourage you to stop, think and consider for a moment what marvellous things He has done for you. Do you know the numerous times that God has sheltered you from jeopardy, and kept you from harm? David declared this in Psalm 3:3, "But thou,

The Reality of My Healing

O LORD, art a shield for me; my glory, and the lifter up of mine head."

Like me, at some point you perhaps despised Him, disrespected Him, and hated Him without a cause; yet His undiluted love toward us never changed. Jesus wants you to surrender all to Him. He is willing to accept you as His own. God is giving you a second chance. Accept it willingly, before it is too late. The love of God is awesome, He sent his son Jesus Christ to die for you and me. Keep John 3:16 in your heart. It says, "for God so loved the world that he gave His only begotten Son that whosoever believeth in him should not perish, but have everlasting life."

There is an abundance of depression, distress, and weariness in this world, as long as you do not have King Jesus. Do not give your life over to the devil, because he will not be afraid to overthrow you when you refuse to submit to him. While living in the world, we are not free from troubling times, difficulties, distress, harassment, unpleasantness, disturbance, or commotion. We are constantly under attack from evil and need divine intervention from God. Whatever the situation, you can call on God. He will not turn His back on you. Matthew 11:28 (NIV) says, "Come to me, all you who are weary and burdened, and I will give you rest."

Salvation is for everyone; there is no discrimination when it comes to Jesus Christ. Whether you secretly or openly ask Him to forgive your sins, He will surely enter your life and make you whole. Invite Jesus to be your personal Saviour, the centre of your life. Revelation 22:17 says, "And the Spirit and

A Special Appeal to Unbelievers

the bride say, Come. And let him that heareth say, Come. And let him that is athirst come. And whosoever will, let him take the water of life freely."

The moment Christ said on the cross, "it is finished" (John 19:30), every person who decides to accept Jesus Christ as his or her personal Saviour, steps into new life. He gave His life for you on the Cross, to rescue you from all iniquity and corruption of this world. Jesus Christ was crucified for your sins and mine, so that we might die to sin and live for righteousness. Through His finished work, we have been set free and healed from our infirmities (1 Peter 2:24).

This may feel like the biggest decision of your life. You must make a choice. We cannot serve two masters at the same time (Matt. 6:24). Either you serve one and despise the other, but choose today who you will serve. Perhaps you are at the end of your rope and there is no hope but to call on the name of the Lord God to save you. What will you do?

You can fulfill the call by just praying one simple prayer: *Lord, please forgive me of every sin that I have committed. I know I am a sinner and I am not worthy of Your grace, but I want to be in deep friendship with You. I want You to correct my faults, and direct my path. Wash me thoroughly and cleanse me from my sins, repair me O Lord and give me a heart of love. In Jesus' name I pray, amen.*

If you said that prayer with sincerity, you are now a child of God. This is just as Scripture tells us, "For whosoever shall call upon the name of the Lord, shall be saved" (Romans 10:13). Get to know God on a greater level starting today!

The Reality of My Healing

Read His Word, take heed to His Word, exercise your faith in His Word and let it mature in your heart. Apply it daily and treasure it as a map for your life. Welcome to the family of God.

Prayer of Healing

Heavenly Father, in the name of Your Son, Jesus Christ, I approach Your mercy seat right now and petition You for healing from this sickness in my body. Lord, I am on the verge of giving up. I ask You Father to give me another touch because I am confident that with just one touch from You, sick bodies are healed, mental faculties restored and souls birthed for Your kingdom. Lord I am asking You to bring solace to my pain and sorrow and to dry all my tears. Hide me under the shadow of Your wings. Let Your healing virtues flow through me even now. Give me the courage and patience to seek Your face. This and other mercies I ask in Jesus Christ's name. Amen!

Author's Biography

Cislyn Tucker has been a Christian for over twenty years. She was nurtured under the Open Bible Standard Churches of Jamaica until 2014 when the Lord directed her to Mystery Church of God Inc. She holds a Diploma in Biblical & Pastoral Studies from the College of Theological and Interdisciplinary Studies (CTIS) and serves passionately in evangelical ministry. She has been married to Junior Tucker for twenty-two (22) years. She currently serves in her local church as President of the Missionary department.

www.ingramcontent.com/pod-product-compliance
Lightning Source LLC
LaVergne TN
LVHW051155080426
835508LV00021B/2640